Editor
Sara Connolly

Editor in Chief
Ina Massler Levin, M.A.

Creative Director
Karen J. Goldfluss, M.S. Ed.

Illustrator
Clint McKnight

Cover Artist
Marilyn Goldberg

Art Coordinator
Renée Mc Elwee

Imaging
James Edward Grace

Publisher

Mary D. Smith, M.S. Ed.

TCR 5906

What's Different?

Grades 1–2

Teacher Created Resources

Author
Christine Smith

Teacher Created Resources
6421 Industry Way
Westminster, CA 92683
www.teachercreated.com
ISBN: 978-1-4206-5906-1

© 2011 Teacher Created Resources
Made in U.S.A.

Teacher Created Resources

Table of Contents

Introduction

The visual puzzles in *Start to Finish: What's Different?* are designed to stimulate thinking skills, support content standards, and entertain students. Each puzzle page presents students with an interesting fact that ties into the classroom curriculum and two pictures to examine. The students are then challenged to look at the pictures carefully and identify what is different.

Visual puzzles that encourage students to identify differences are more than just fun activities. They reinforce and stimulate critical-thinking and problem-solving skills. As students solve the puzzles, they are improving their observation skills and attention to detail. Their brains are learning to evaluate and analyze visual data through comparison. Students can also work on their fine-motor skills and eye-hand coordination by coloring the pictures.

The puzzles in this book can be used in learning centers, as extension activities, for students who finish early, and as at-home enrichment activities. Have fun learning!

Matter of Fact

Steam, an ice cube, and a lake are all forms of water. Water, like all matter, can be a solid, liquid, or a gas.

Look at these pictures. Circle 5 things that are different in the picture above.

Brrr!

Animals and plants can be found all over the world, including Antarctica, the coldest place on Earth.

Look at these pictures. Circle 5 things that are different in the picture above.

It's a Jungle

Over half of the plant and animal species on Earth live in rain forests.

Look at these pictures. Circle 5 things that are different in the picture above.

Timber!

Coast redwoods are the world's tallest trees. They can grow to over 300 feet tall and live for over 2,000 years.

Look at these pictures. Circle 5 things that are different in the picture above.

Rain or Shine?

Scientists called meteorologists use space satellites to study, track, and predict weather.

Look at these pictures. Circle 5 things that are different in the picture above.

Strike Up the Band

Sound is made when an object vibrates. For example, a person strums the strings of a guitar to make them vibrate and create music.

Look at these pictures. Circle 5 things that are different in the picture above.

Falling for Gravity

The next time you fall and scrape your knee, blame gravity. Gravity is the force that makes things fall to the ground.

Look at these pictures. Circle 5 things that are different in the picture above.

Get Moving

Need to move something? You will need to use force. Force means pushing or pulling on an object. Force makes things move.

Look at these pictures. Circle 5 things that are different in the picture above.

Eggs to Legs

Frogs lay clumps of eggs that hatch into tadpoles. The tadpoles grow legs and lose their tails as they become adult frogs that can live on land.

Look at these pictures. Circle 5 things that are different in the picture above.

Dirty Business

Paleontologists study fossils found in the layers of the Earth's surface to learn about animals and plants from the past.

Look at these pictures. Circle 5 things that are different in the picture above.

Tiny Rocks

Sand is made as rocks are broken down into smaller and smaller pieces through a process called weathering.

Look at these pictures. Circle 5 things that are different in the picture above.

Recycling

It takes as little as 60 days for a soda can to go from the recycling bin back to the store shelf as a new can.

Look at these pictures. Circle 5 things that are different in the picture above.

Computers

Early computers were hard to use, slow, and so big that they filled entire rooms. Now, we have computers that are easy to use, fast, and small enough to fit in a pocket.

Look at these pictures. Circle 5 things that are different in the picture above.

16

Every Vote Counts

Citizens in democratic countries, like the United States, get to vote for their leaders.

Look at these pictures. Circle 5 things that are different in the picture above.

Welcome

The Statue of Liberty in New York City is a symbol of freedom. It has welcomed over 12 million immigrants to the United States.

Look at these pictures. Circle 5 things that are different in the picture above.

Fourth of July

On July 4, 1776, the United States declared their independence from Great Britain. Americans celebrate this event every July 4th with parties and fireworks.

Look at these pictures. Circle 5 things that are different in the picture above.

Time for School

A hundred years ago, most students went to school in one-room schoolhouses. One teacher would teach students at many different grade levels.

Look at these pictures. Circle 5 things that are different in the picture above.

Giddy-up!

Before the invention of cars, people traveled long distances by horseback, horse-drawn wagon, or train.

Look at these pictures. Circle 5 things that are different in the picture above.

Who Was First?

American Indians lived all across North America long before it was discovered by Columbus.

Look at these pictures. Circle 5 things that are different in the picture above.

I'll Trade You

Before the use of money, people traded goods and services for what they needed. This was called bartering.

Look at these pictures. Circle 5 things that are different in the picture above.

Euros, Dollars, and Yen

Different countries use different currencies. Currency is another word for money.

Look at these pictures. Circle 5 things that are different in the picture above.

Set Sail

Cargo ships carry food, toys, computers, and other goods from where they were made to countries that want to buy them.

Look at these pictures. Circle 5 things that are different in the picture above.

Ties to the Past

Ancestors are the family members who lived before us. Their journals and photos are a good way to learn about life in the past.

Look at these pictures. Circle 5 things that are different in the picture above.

Where We Live

Areas where few people live are called rural areas. Places where lots of
people live are called urban areas.

Look at these pictures. Circle 5 things that are different in the picture above.

Real Heroes

Real heroes make the world better by their actions. For example, President Abraham Lincoln ended slavery in the United States.

Look at these pictures. Circle 5 things that are different in the picture above.

Dollars and Cents

Did you know that coins stay in circulation for about 30 years? A one-dollar bill only lasts about 18 months.

Look at these pictures. Circle 5 things that are different in the picture above.

What Time Is It?

People in Egypt used sundials to tell time 3,500 years ago. Clocks like the ones we use today were not invented until about 335 years ago.

Look at these pictures. Circle 5 things that are different in the picture above.

Street Shapes

The next time you are riding in the car, see how many different types of street signs you can find. Each type is a different shape and color.

Look at these pictures. Circle 5 things that are different in the picture above.

Yummy Fractions

Mrs. Green cut the cakes for the bake sale. When a whole is divided into equal parts, it is divided into fractions.

Look at these pictures. Circle 5 things that are different in the picture above.

Ticket Please

Prices do not stay the same over time. For example, the average price for a movie ticket was $3.55 in 1985 and $7.50 in 2009.

Look at these pictures. Circle 5 things that are different in the picture above.

Pyramids

Geometric shapes can be found all around us, including in buildings. The pyramids in Egypt are an example of this.

Look at these pictures. Circle 5 things that are different in the picture above.

Tangrams

A tangram is a Chinese puzzle. Each piece is a geometric shape. The goal is to use all seven pieces to make different shapes or pictures.

Look at these pictures. Circle 5 things that are different in the picture above.

How Far?

Most of the world measures distance in meters. The United States measures distance in feet. One meter is a little bit longer than three feet.

Look at these pictures. Circle 5 things that are different in the picture above.

In the Balance

A balance scale compares what two things weigh. The end that is down is the heaviest. The end that is up is the lightest.

Look at these pictures. Circle 5 things that are different in the picture above.

Words and Pictures

An author writes the words in a book, and an illustrator draws the pictures. Some people do both, like Eric Carle. He is the author and illustrator of *The Very Hungry Caterpillar*.

Look at these pictures. Circle 5 things that are different in the picture above.

Playground Rhymes

Rhyming words have the same ending sound and are used in poems, songs, and chants. For example, "Teddy bear, teddy bear, touch the ground. Teddy bear, teddy bear, turn around."

Look at these pictures. Circle 5 things that are different in the picture above.

In the Woods

"Little Red Riding Hood" takes place in the woods. This is called the setting of the story.

Look at these pictures. Circle 5 things that are different in the picture above.

A Writer's Best Friend

A **dictionary** is a writer's best friend because it gives the correct spellings of words and their meanings.

Look at these pictures. Circle 5 things that are different in the picture above.

Check It Out!

There are over 9,000 public libraries in the United States. When was the last time you visited the library?

Look at these pictures. Circle 5 things that are different in the picture above.

In the News

Many people read the newspaper every day. Newspapers give readers information about what is happening in the world.

Look at these pictures. Circle 5 things that are different in the picture above.

Special Delivery

The U.S. Postal Service handles around 667 million pieces of mail every day, including almost half of the world's cards and letters.

Look at these pictures. Circle 5 things that are different in the picture above.

Real or Not?

Nonfiction books describe things that are real. Fiction books tell stories that are not real.

Look at these pictures. Circle 5 things that are different in the picture above.

The Main Character

The main character is the person or animal the story is about. For example, the gingerbread man is the main character of "The Gingerbread Man."

Look at these pictures. Circle 5 things that are different in the picture above.

Comic Strips

Comics are a popular part of newspapers. A comic strip tells a short story using drawings and speech bubbles.

Look at these pictures. Circle 5 things that are different in the picture above.

Strong Bones

There are over 200 bones in the human body. Milk helps keep them strong by providing the calcium they need.

Look at these pictures. Circle 5 things that are different in the picture above.

Sweet Dreams

Sleep is important for learning and staying healthy. You will spend about $\frac{1}{3}$ of your life sleeping.

Look at these pictures. Circle 5 things that are different in the picture above.

Play Safely

A helmet helps protect your brain. So the next time you want to have some fun on wheels, be sure to strap on your helmet.

Look at these pictures. Circle 5 things that are different in the picture above.

Smile!

Tooth enamel protects your teeth from cavities. It is harder than bone, but it will become weak if it is not taken care of.

Look at these pictures. Circle 5 things that are different in the picture above.

Achoo!

When you have a cold, cough and sneeze into your arm, not your hands.
This helps stop the spread of germs.

Look at these pictures. Circle 5 things that are different in the picture above.

An Apple a Day

An apple a day may keep the doctor away, but washing your hands works even **better**. Be sure to always wash your hands before eating and after going to the bathroom.

Look at these pictures. Circle 5 things that are different in the picture above.

53   *#5906 Start to Finish: What's Different?*

Sun Safety

The sun gives us heat and light, but it can also hurt our skin and eyes.
Protect yourself with sunscreen and sunglasses.

Look at these pictures. Circle 5 things that are different in the picture above.

Hungry?

A healthy diet is made up of different types of foods, including fruits and vegetables. Try to eat a variety of fruits and vegetables every day.

Look at these pictures. Circle 5 things that are different in the picture above.

Get Moving

Run! Jump! Climb! Dance! Play! It's all exercise, and it's all good for you.
Try to get moving at least 60 minutes every day.

Look at these pictures. Circle 5 things that are different in the picture above.

Breakfast Time

It's true! Breakfast is the most important meal of the day. It gives you the fuel you need to learn and stay alert at school.

Look at these pictures. Circle 5 things that are different in the picture above.

Answer Key

Page 4

Page 8

Page 5

Page 9

Page 6

Page 10

Page 7

Page 11

Answer Key *(cont.)*

Page 12

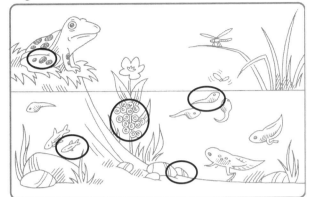

Page 13

Page 14

Page 15

Page 16

Page 17

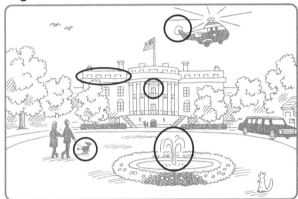

Page 18

Page 19

Answer Key *(cont.)*

Page 20

Page 21

Page 22

Page 23

Page 24

Page 25

Page 26

Page 27

Answer Key *(cont.)*

Page 28

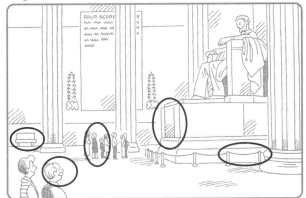

Page 29

Page 30

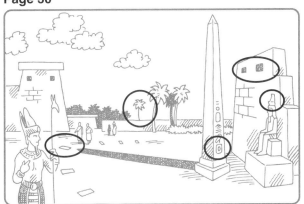

Page 31

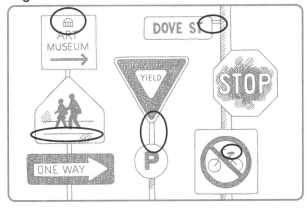

Page 32

Page 33

Page 34

Page 35

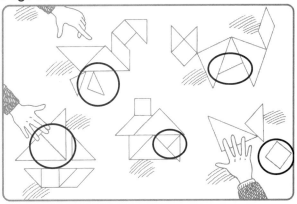

Answer Key *(cont.)*

Page 36

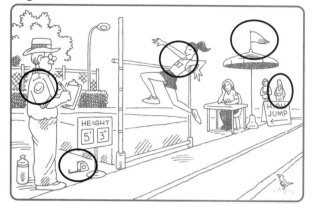

Page 37

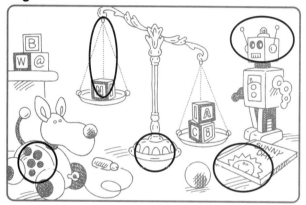

Page 38

Page 39

Page 40

Page 41

Page 42

Page 43

Answer Key *(cont.)*

Page 44

Page 48

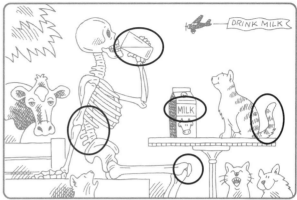

Page 45

Page 49

Page 46

Page 50

Page 47

Page 51

Answer Key (cont.)

Page 52

Page 53

Page 54

Page 55

Page 56

Page 57